Melinda Bula

candy cane lane

Quilts and More to Sweeten the Holidays

Martingale®
& COMPANY

Candy Cane Lane:
Quilts and More to Sweeten the Holidays
© 2009 by Melinda Bula

That Patchwork Place® is an imprint
of Martingale & Company®.

Martingale & Company
20205 144th Ave. NE
Woodinville, WA 98072-8478 USA
www.martingale-pub.com

Printed in China
14 13 12 11 10 09   8 7 6 5 4 3 2 1

Library of Congress Cataloging-in-Publication Data
Library of Congress Control Number: 2009017857

ISBN: 978-1-56477-924-3

Credits

President & CEO: *Tom Wierzbicki*
Editor in Chief: *Mary V. Green*
Managing Editor: *Tina Cook*
Technical Editor: *Laurie Baker*
Copy Editor: *Sheila Chapman Ryan*
Design Director: *Stan Green*
Production Manager: *Regina Girard*
Illustrator: *Robin Strobel*
Cover & Text Designer: *Adrienne Smitke*
Photographer: *Brent Kane*

Dedication

To my creative designer mother, Lavonna Hopkins, who created holiday magic each year for my sisters and me on a very limited budget. Her doors were always open to strangers and friends alike, and she set the finest table to welcome them all. She showed the true meaning of Christmas with her love of the Lord and would never let us forget what Christmas was about. Thanks, Mom, for giving me the desire to make gifts and patterns for others.

Mission Statement
Dedicated to providing quality products
and service to inspire creativity.

Contents

Welcome to Candy Cane Lane

Christmas is full of family traditions. I remember how my mother would create a new Christmas theme each year. The amazing thing was that she would start with the previous year's decorations, purchase a few new ones, and then arrange them differently to create a whole new look. My most vivid memory of one new item was the year we got a blue tree—and this was long before Martha Stewart's influence! I try and keep the tradition alive by adding a few new decorations to my family's stash each year, too.

Another tradition I looked forward to when I was growing up was hanging the Christmas stockings. My sisters and I were always excited when Mom would bring out the stockings she had made for us. They were covered with beads and sequins and would sparkle in the light cast by the tree. I thought they were so fancy. She recently gave us those childhood stockings and it instantly brought back those wonderful memories.

Mom always tried to make us something special each year, too. One year, after she and dad had tucked us into bed, I heard the hum of her sewing machine late into the night. That year we all received handmade Annie dolls with complete wardrobes, including shoes! How she did this I will never know, but I treasure that doll to this day. It was such a fun gift!

I feel so fortunate to have memories of Christmas to cherish. I hope that the quilt and coordinating projects in this book will bring your family joy and excitement each year you pull them out to decorate for the holiday season.

From my family to yours, Merry Christmas!

~Melinda

General Instructions

Before you begin any of the projects in this book, be sure to read though the project instructions. I love to try new techniques, and I don't always do things the same way from project to project. This section will go over some of the specific techniques I use and supplies I recommend so that you can create your new holiday memories.

Selecting and Preparing Fabrics

A Christmas project does not have to be made out of Christmas fabrics. When I designed the "Candy Cane Lane" quilt and coordinating projects, I knew that I didn't want to use the same old traditional reds and greens. I began by looking for inspiration in old Christmas magazines and when I found some things that caught my eye, I tore out the pages and took them to my fabric stash and began pulling out the colors that I saw. The colors were different, but that's why I loved them. Let your eyes and your emotions guide you when picking your fabrics, and if they lead you toward something untraditional, it's OK. There is a world of options outside of the Christmas aisle. Just be sure you select good-quality 100%-cotton fabrics

for the best results, and wash, dry, and press them before you begin. Do not use fabric softener in the washer or the dryer, especially if the fabrics will be used for fusible-web appliqué pieces.

Appliqué Methods

I have included instructions for two appliqué techniques. If you are more comfortable with another method, feel free to use it. You may also prefer to use a combination of methods within a project, and that is perfectly fine as well.

Take the time to read the instructions for each project before you begin. They are all put together differently; sometimes the appliqué is done first and sometimes the embellishments are applied before the appliqués. All of the appliqué patterns can be found on the pullout pattern sheet in the back of the book. Patterns do not include seam allowances.

Background pieces on which the appliqués are stitched are cut larger than needed and trimmed to the correct size after the motifs have been stitched in place. Keep this in mind as you position the appliqués so that you do not risk capturing them in the seam allowance or cutting them off when you trim the piece to size.

Fusible-Web Appliqué

I love this method! It's a great time saver and with today's advances in fusible products and sewing-machine technology, you can produce appliqués that look close to hand stitched. I prefer to use Steam-A-Seam 2 because it's a double-stick, pressure-sensitive fusible web, which means it's sticky on both sides. This allows me to temporarily stick the appliqué in place on the background before permanently fusing it in place. If you choose to use Steam-A-Seam 2, follow the instructions that come with the product; follow the general instructions below for all other fusible-web products, referring to the product instructions for specifics.

1. Trace the appliqué patterns onto a sheet of tracing paper. Roughly cut around the shapes.
2. Follow the manufacturer's instructions to fuse the fusible web to the wrong side of the appropriate fabrics. Pin the patterns to the right side of the appropriate fabrics. Cut out the appliqués on the marked lines.
3. Remove the paper backing and position the appliqués on the background fabric in the order indicated; fuse in place.
4. Using a straight stitch and matching thread, machine stitch close to the edge around each appliqué to permanently secure it. You can also use a narrow zigzag stitch, blanket stitch, or other decorative stitch if you prefer.

Needle-Turn Appliqué

This is the method I used for the main quilt project. It takes a little more time than fusible-web appliqué, but it provides the look I prefer for projects I want to become heirlooms.

1. Make a template for each shape needed. To do this, use an ultrafine-tip Sharpie marker to trace the appliqué patterns onto the dull side of a piece of freezer paper or template plastic. Template plastic is a better choice when you need several of the same shape. Cut out the shapes on the drawn lines with paper scissors.
2. If you are using freezer-paper templates, iron them to the right side of the appropriate fabrics, shiny side down. Leave at least ½" of space between shapes. Trace around them with a fine-tip marker or a chalk pencil. For template-plastic templates, hold them in place on the right side of the appropriate fabric and trace around them.
3. Remove the templates. Cut around each shape, adding a ¼" seam allowance.

4. Pin or use water-soluble glue, such as Roxanne's Glue-Baste-It, to baste piece 1 in place.
5. Use the point of the needle to turn under a short length of the seam allowance. With a size 10 or 11 straw needle and matching thread, hand appliqué the turned-under portion in place. Continue around the shape in this manner.

6. Baste and stitch the remaining pieces to the background fabric in numerical order. You do not need to turn under seam allowances that will be covered by another piece.

Embellishments

The projects in this book are a wonderful place to add Christmas sparkle and "bling," and I encourage you to add whatever fancy touches make you feel good. Gather a selection of crystals, beads, buttons, ribbons, and trims and let your mind go wild with the possibilities. Embellishments are done at different times, depending on the project, so be sure to read the instructions carefully before you begin.

Hot-Fix Crystals

Hot-fix crystals are one of my favorites for adding sparkle to projects. You'll need a special applicator for adhering them to the fabric, but it is well worth the investment. There are many sources for hot-fix crystals on the Internet if you can't find them locally.

Sequins

Sequins are another good embellishment for adding a bit of glitz. Hand stitch them to your project with thread that matches the sequins, using a small seed bead to hold them in place. Come up through the fabric at the desired location, go through the hole in the sequin, through the hole in the bead, and then back down through the hole in the sequin and through the fabric. Knot the thread on the back of your fabric when you are finished.

Eyelets

Small eyelets are great for lending a realistic touch to the Christmas tags. They come in many sizes and colors, and you can find them in most craft and scrapbook stores. You will need an eyelet setter and a small hammer to apply them.

Embroidery Stitches

Embroidery stitches are used to embellish some of the quilt blocks and other projects in this book. Each pattern will give you suggestions for which stitches to use. Some basic stitches are shown below. Work the stitches using two strands of embroidery floss and a size 8 embroidery needle unless otherwise indicated.

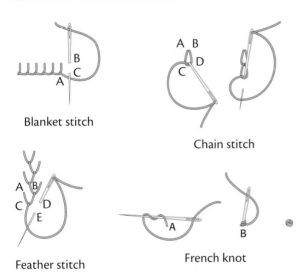

Blanket stitch

Chain stitch

Feather stitch

French knot

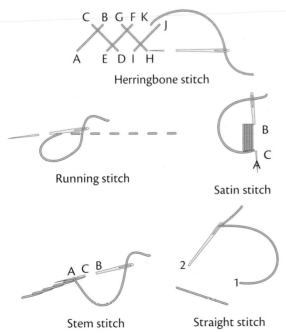

Herringbone stitch

Running stitch

Satin stitch

Stem stitch

Straight stitch

Lettering

Several of the blocks in the quilt contain lettering. The letters can be added using your favorite appliqué technique, or you can embroider them by hand or machine. If you prefer hand embroidery, use a satin stitch (shown at left). For machine embroidery, either free-motion stitch the letters or use a built-in font on your machine, if available, or an alphabet from an embroidery disk.

Yo-Yos

Yo-yos are fun! I've used them to embellish the outer border of the quilt and the edges of the "Candy Cane Table Runner," but you could substitute them anywhere a round piece is needed (think berries and ornaments).

1. Use the pattern on pullout 4 to make a template from template plastic.
2. Place the template on the wrong side of the desired fabric and trace around it with a pencil or an ultrafine-tip marker. Cut out the shape on the drawn line.
3. Finger-press a ¼" seam allowance to the wrong side, all around the yo-yo.
4. Thread a hand-sewing needle with quilting thread; knot the ends together.
5. Baste the seam allowance around the circle using a large gathering stitch. Pull gently on the threads to gather the fabric circle. Take a couple of stitches to secure the gathers; then knot and trim your thread. Flatten the yo-yo with your fingers and evenly distribute the gathers, if necessary.

Candy Cane Lane Quilt

This cheery Christmas quilt is made with 10 different blocks. Instructions for each block are given separately so that you can make the quilt as shown or mix and match the blocks as desired. Appliqué patterns and placement guides are given on the pullout pattern section.

Finished quilt size: 51" x 60½"

Block 1—Snow Family

Finished block size: 9½" x 19"

Materials

11" x 20" rectangle of yellow fabric for block background

¼ yard *total* of assorted white fabrics for bodies

Scraps of assorted fabrics for hats, apron, bow, broom, noses, and cheeks

Red embroidery thread, floss, or fabric for letters (material will depend on your preferred method)

Embroidery floss: brown, black, and pink

Buttons: 3 small round for Snow Dad; 5 small round for Snow Boy; 1 heart for Snow Mom

Brown, black, and pink ultrafine-tip permanent markers

Making the Block

The appliqué patterns and a placement guide are given on page 1 of the pullout pattern section.

1. Refer to "Appliqué Methods" on page 5 to prepare the appliqué shapes from the appropriate fabrics using your preferred method.

2. Fold the yellow rectangle in half vertically and horizontally; finger-press the folds to mark the center. Open up the rectangle and appliqué the shapes in place in numerical order.

3. Use the markers to transfer the stitching details to the rectangle, using black for the eyes and mouth, brown for the arms and fingers, and pink for the apron strings. Refer to "Lettering" on page 7 to appliqué or to hand or machine embroider the letters. Refer to "Embroidery Stitches" on page 7 and use two strands of black floss to work French knots for the eyes and mouths; use three strands of brown floss to stem stitch the arms and fingers and three strands of pink floss to stem stitch the apron strings.

4. Stitch the buttons in place where indicated on the pattern.

5. Trim the rectangle to 10" x 19½", keeping the design centered.

Block 2—Snowflake 1

Finished block size: 9½" x 9½"

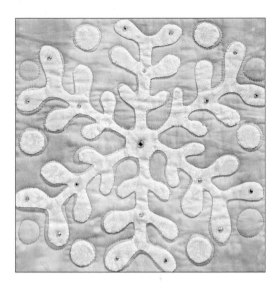

Materials

11" x 11" square of light blue fabric for block background

⅜ yard of white fabric for snowflake

19 hot-fix crystals or crystal beads

Making the Block

The appliqué patterns are given on page 1 of the pullout pattern section.

1. Refer to "Appliqué Methods" on page 5 to prepare the appliqué shapes from the white fabric using your preferred method.

2. Fold the light blue square in half horizontally and vertically; finger-press the folds to mark the center. Open up the square and appliqué the shapes in place in numerical order.

3. Trim the block to 10" x 10", keeping the design centered. The crystals or beads will be applied after the quilt has been quilted.

Block 3—Stocking

Finished block size: 9½" x 19"

Materials

11" x 20" rectangle of turquoise fabric for block
    background
½ yard of red print for stocking body
¼ yard of white fabric for stocking cuff
¼ yard of yellow fabric for stars
Scrap of ribbon or fabric for cuff band
Scrap of blue fabric for cuff pom-poms
Red embroidery thread, floss, or fabric for initial
    (material will depend on your preferred method)
1 package of white jumbo rickrack
Chalk pencil

Making the Block

The appliqué patterns are given on page 1 of the pullout
pattern section.

1. Trace the cuff pattern onto the right side of the white
    fabric using the chalk pencil. Leave enough space
    around the cuff shape when you trace it to insert the
    fabric into an embroidery hoop if you will be hand or
    machine embroidering the initial. Refer to "Lettering"
    on page 7 to appliqué or to hand or machine embroi-
    der the desired initial to the cuff. Refer to "Appliqué
    Methods" on page 5 to apply the band to the top of
    the cuff using your preferred method. Prepare the cuff
    for appliqué using your preferred method.

2. Refer to "Appliqué Methods" to prepare the remaining
    appliqué shapes from the appropriate fabrics using
    your preferred method.

3. Press the stocking seam allowance under ¼". On the
    wrong side of the stocking shape, baste the rickrack
    around all of the edges but the top, allowing half of
    the rickrack to be visible from the right side.

4. Fold the turquoise rectangle in half vertically and
    horizontally; finger-press the folds to mark the center.
    Open up the rectangle and pin the stocking appliqué
    in place. Appliqué the stocking in place through all
    the layers.

5. Position the prepared cuff at the top of the stocking
    and appliqué it in place. Appliqué a pom-pom (shape
    3) to each point on the cuff. Continue appliquéing the
    shapes in place in the order indicated.

6. Trim the rectangle to 10" x 19½", keeping the design
    centered.

Block 4—House

Finished block size: 9½" x 19"

Materials

11" x 20" rectangle of dark blue fabric for block background

¼ yard of dark green fabric for house

¼ yard of red fabric for roof

¼ yard of light green fabric for stars

⅛ yard of lime green fabric for door

⅛ yard of medium blue fabric for door and window frames

⅛ yard of white for snow

⅛ yard of gold #1 for windows

Scrap of gold #2 for chimney

Scrap of red print for heart on door

1 package of assorted red glass seed beads for Christmas lights around roof

20 pink hot-fix crystals OR sequins and seed beads for sky

Making the Block

The appliqué patterns are given on page 1 of the pullout pattern section.

1. Prepare the window and door appliqués.
   For needle-turn appliqué, trace the door and window appliqués onto freezer paper to make templates. Cut out the window and door openings along the dashed lines. Press each freezer-paper shape onto the right side of the medium blue fabric, leaving at least ½" of space between each shape. Trace around the outside of each shape and inside the window and door openings. Remove the freezer-paper templates. Cut out each piece, adding a ¼" seam allowance. Cut from corner to corner in both directions inside the openings marked by the dotted lines, cutting up to but not through the corners. Fold the fabric inside the marked areas to the wrong side; press. For the windows, cut a piece of gold fabric #1 slightly larger than the blue pieces and place it behind each window frame so that the right side is showing through the openings. Do the same with the green fabric for the door. Appliqué around the openings.

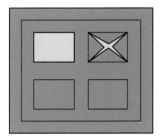

   For fusible-web appliqué, trace the window and door shapes onto the paper side of the fusible web, including the inner dashed lines. Roughly cut around each shape and fuse them to the wrong side of the medium blue fabric. Cut each piece out on the drawn lines, including the inner dashed lines. Remove the paper backing from each piece. Apply fusible web to a piece of gold fabric large enough to accommodate all three windows and to a piece of lime green fabric slightly larger than the door. Do not remove the paper backing. Fuse the blue window shapes to the *right side* of the prepared gold fabric and the door shape to the *right side* of the prepared lime green fabric. Cut around the edges of each window piece and the door piece.

2. Refer to "Appliqué Methods" on page 5 to prepare the remaining appliqué shapes from the appropriate fabrics using your preferred method.

3. Fold the dark blue rectangle in half vertically and horizontally; finger-press the folds to mark the center. Open up the rectangle and appliqué the shapes in place in numerical order, randomly placing the stars in the sky above the house.

4. Trim the rectangle to 10" x 19½", keeping the design centered. The crystals and beads will be applied after the quilt has been quilted.

Block 5—Christmas Tree

Finished block size: 9½" x 19"

Materials

½ yard of light green fabric for block background
½ yard of medium light green fabric for block background
½ yard of white fabric for tree
Scraps of assorted red and blue prints for ornaments
Scrap of yellow fabric for star
1 yard of green ¼"-wide bias tape for tree stand
Multicolored square sequins and matching seed beads for embellishing
Chalk pencil

Making the Block

The appliqué patterns are given on page 2 of the pullout pattern section.

1. From each of the light green and medium light green fabrics, cut four strips, 2" x 11". With the colors alternating, sew the strips together along the long edges. Press the seam allowances in one direction. Trim the pieced rectangle to 11" x 20".
2. Refer to "Appliqué Methods" on page 5 to prepare the appliqué shapes from the appropriate fabrics using your preferred method.

3. Fold the pieced rectangle in half vertically and horizontally; finger-press the folds to mark the center. Open up the rectangle. Using the chalk pencil, transfer the placement marks for the tree stand to the rectangle. Appliqué the seam binding over the lines, and then appliqué the remaining shapes in place in numerical order.
4. Trim the rectangle to 10" x 19½". The sequins and seed beads will be stitched in place after the quilt has been quilted.

Block 6—Snowflake 2

Finished block size: 9½" x 9½"

Materials

11" x 11" square of medium blue fabric for block background
⅜ yard of white fabric for snowflake
18 hot-fix crystals or beads

Making the Block

The appliqué patterns are given on page 2 of the pullout pattern section.

1. Refer to "Appliqué Methods" on page 5 to prepare the appliqué shapes from the white fabric using your preferred method.
2. Fold the medium blue square in half horizontally and vertically; finger-press the folds to mark the center. Open up the square and appliqué the shapes in place in numerical order.
3. Trim the block to 10" x 10", keeping the design centered. The crystals or beads will be applied after the quilt has been quilted.

Block 7—Christmas Tags

Finished block size: 9½" x 19"

Materials

11" x 20" rectangle of light turquoise for background
½ yard of tan print for tags
2 yards of brown ¼"-wide bias tape for clothesline
Embroidery floss: variegated green for pine boughs,
    white for tag strings
Green embroidery thread, floss, or fabric for letters
    (material will depend on your preferred method)
14 small brass eyelets
Template plastic
Green ultrafine-tip permanent marker
Chalk pencil

Making the Block

The appliqué patterns and a placement guide are given on page 2 of the pullout pattern section.

1. Fold the light turquoise rectangle in half vertically and horizontally; finger-press the folds to mark the center. Open up the rectangle. Following the placement guide on the pullout pattern section, use the chalk pencil to transfer the clothesline placement lines to the rectangle. Appliqué the brown bias tape to the drawn lines.

2. Trace the tag pattern onto template plastic and cut it out. Using the template and the chalk pencil, trace 14 shapes onto the right side of the tan print, leaving enough room between each tag for seam allowance. Refer to "Lettering" on page 7 to appliqué or to hand or machine embroider a letter to each tag to spell *Merry Christmas*.

3. Refer to "Appliqué Methods" on page 5 to prepare the tags for appliqué using your preferred method. Follow the manufacturer's instructions to apply an eyelet to the top of each tag where indicated on the pattern. Appliqué the tags to the light turquoise rectangle along the bias tape clothesline so that they spell *Merry Christmas*, referring to the photo if necessary for placement.

4. Use the cutting guide on the pullout pattern section to cut four pieces of bias tape for the clothesline tails. Appliqué the tails to the ends of the clothesline.

5. Using the green marker and referring to the photo, mark the placement of the pine boughs. You can use any of the pine bough patterns that you wish, flipping and rotating them as needed to achieve the desired effect. Refer to "Embroidery Stitches" on page 7 and use two strands of variegated green floss to work a running stitch for the stems, and then straight stitch each needle.

6. Trim the rectangle to 10" x 19½", keeping the design centered. The tag "string" ties will be added after the quilt has been quilted.

Block 8—Flowers

Finished block size: 9½" x 28½"

Materials

11" x 30" rectangle of golden yellow fabric for
  block background
½ yard of red fabric for outer flowers
¼ yard *total* of 3 assorted green fabrics for leaves
  and stems
⅛ yard of yellow for flower centers
⅛ yard of reddish orange for inner flowers
1 package of white jumbo rickrack

Making the Block

The appliqué patterns are given on page 2 of the pullout
pattern section.

1. Refer to "Appliqué Methods" on page 5 to prepare
   the appliqué shapes from the appropriate fabrics
   using your preferred method. Press under the inner-
   flower seam allowance ¼".

2. On the wrong side of the inner-flower shapes, baste
   the rickrack around the edge, allowing half of the rickrack to be visible from the right side.

3. Fold the golden yellow rectangle in half vertically and
   horizontally; finger-press the folds to mark the center.
   Open up the rectangle and appliqué the shapes in
   place in numerical order.

4. Trim the rectangle to 10" x 29", keeping the design
   centered.

Block 9— Candy Canes

Finished block size:
10" x 47½"

Materials

11" x 49" strip of turquoise
  fabric for block background
½ yard of red fabric for candy
  cane stripes
½ yard of white fabric for candy
  cane bodies
½ yard of green print for bows
Scraps of a different green print
  for bow centers
2 yards of ¼"-wide red double-
  faced silk ribbon for bow
  centers
9 small brass jingle bells for
  bow centers

Making the Block

The appliqué patterns are given
on page 3 of the pullout pattern
section.

1. Refer to "Appliqué Methods" on page 5 to
   prepare the appliqué
   shapes from the appro-
   priate fabrics using your
   preferred method. You will
   need enough shapes for three candy cane/bow sets,
   reversing the pieces for two of the sets.

2. Referring to the photo, position the shape 1 pieces on
   the turquoise strip, leaving an equal amount of space
   between the candy canes and at the top and bottom
   of the strip. Using your preferred method, appliqué the
   shapes in place and then add the red stripes in order
   as indicated. Appliqué the bows in place at about the
   center of each candy cane.

3. Trim the strip to 10½" x 48", keeping the design
   centered. The block will be embellished with the red
   ribbon and jingle bells after the quilt has been quilted.

Blocks 10 and 11—
Holly and Berries

Finished block size: 9½" x 47½"

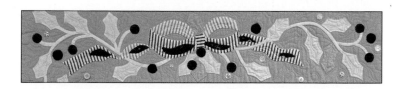

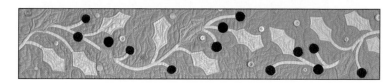

Materials

1⅜ yards of bluish green fabric for block backgrounds

½ yard of red-and-white striped fabric for bow

¼ yard of red print for bow shading

½ yard of lime green fabric for holly leaves

1⅝ yards of pale lime green fabric for holly leaves and vines

¼ yard *total* of 2 different red fabrics for berries

30 assorted white pearl and/or plastic buttons

⅜" bias bar

Making the Blocks

The appliqué patterns are given on page 3 of the pullout pattern section.

1. From the bluish green fabric, cut two rectangles, 11" x 49".

2. Refer to "Appliqué Methods" on page 5 to prepare the appliqué shapes from the appropriate fabrics using your preferred method. I used the wrong side of the red-and-white striped fabric for pieces 3, 4, and 5.

3. From the remainder of the pale lime green fabric, cut 1¼"-wide bias strips to make the vine. You will need approximately 6 yards total of finished vine in various lengths. To make the vines, fold each strip in half, wrong sides together, and stitch ⅛" from the long raw edges to form a tube. Insert the bias bar into the tube, roll the seam to the underside, and press flat. Remove the bias bar.

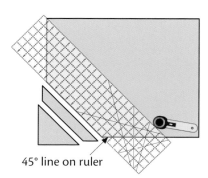

45° line on ruler

Stitch ⅛" from edges.

Bias bar

4. Fold one bluish green rectangle in half vertically and horizontally; finger-press the folds to mark the center. This will be the top border strip. Open up the rectangle. Referring to the photo, pin or glue-baste the vine pieces and the bow pieces to this piece, centering the bow. Position the vines on the remaining rectangle. Keep in mind that the vine ends will be covered by leaves and berries and that the finished size of each rectangle will be 9½" x 47½". One vine will cross over the seam that joins the side and top rectangles. Set this vine aside and then appliqué the remaining vines and bow pieces in place using your preferred method. Position the leaves on the rectangles and appliqué them in place, again removing and setting aside the leaf between the two rectangles and at the ends of the set-aside vine. Add the berries last.

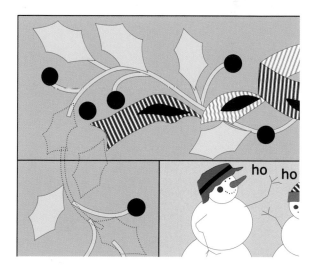

5. Before you trim the rectangles, pin them together just as they will be joined on the quilt. You will be better able to determine where to trim if you do this. Make any necessary adjustments, and then trim the rectangles to 10" x 48". The button embellishments will be added after the quilt has been quilted.

Quilt Construction

Now that your blocks are done, it's time to put them together and complete your quilt. This quilt is meant to be hung; be sure to add a hanging sleeve so you can display it on a wall for all to enjoy during the holiday season.

Materials

4 yards of fabric for backing (crosswise seam) and hanging sleeve

1 yard *total* of at least 8 assorted fabrics for yo-yos (use leftover fabrics from your finished blocks or use completely different fabrics; the more variety, the better)

½ yard of white fabric for yo-yo border

⅝ yard of fabric for binding

55" x 64" piece of batting

Template plastic

Assembling the Quilt Top

1. Arrange blocks 1–8 into rows. Sew the blocks in each row together. Press the seam allowances in the directions shown. Sew the rows together. Add block 9 to the right side of the joined blocks and block 10 to the left side of the joined blocks. Press the seam allowances toward blocks 9 and 10. Join block 11 to the top of the quilt. Press the seam allowance toward block 11.

2. Appliqué the vine and leaves that you removed earlier to blocks 10 and 11 using your preferred method.

3. From the white fabric for the yo-yo border, cut five strips, 2¼" wide x the width of the fabric. Join the strips end to end to make one long strip. Measure the length of the quilt top through the center. From the pieced strip, cut two strips to this measurement and join them to the sides of the quilt top. Press the seam

allowances toward the border strips. Measure the width of the quilt top through the center, including the side borders you just added. From the remainder of the pieced strip, cut two strips to this measurement and join them to the top and bottom of the quilt top. Press the seam allowances toward the border strips.

Finishing the Quilt

1. Piece the quilt backing so that it is 4" to 6" longer and wider than the quilt top. Layer the quilt top with batting and backing and baste the layers together. Hand or machine quilt as desired. Trim the batting and backing even with the quilt top.

2. Make a hanging sleeve. Measure the width of the quilt top and cut a piece of fabric 10" wide x the width of your quilt. Press the short ends of the strip under ½" twice. Stitch the hem in place.

3. Press the hemmed sleeve in half lengthwise, wrong sides together.

4. With the raw edges aligned, center the sleeve at the top of your quilt. Pin it in place. Using your walking foot, baste the sleeve in place. The sleeve will be caught in the seam allowance when the quilt is bound.

5. From the binding fabric, cut six 2½"-wide strips and join them with a diagonal seam to make one long strip. Trim the seam allowances to ¼" and press them open.

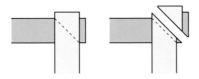

6. Cut one end of the pieced strip at a 45° angle and press it under ¼". Press the strip in half lengthwise, wrong sides together.

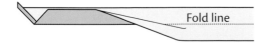

Fold line

7. Beginning with the angled end, pin the binding to one edge of the front side of the quilt. Using your walking foot and a ¼" seam allowance, stitch the binding to the first side, beginning about 8" from the angled end and ending ¼" from the first corner. Backstitch, remove the quilt from under the needle, and clip the threads.

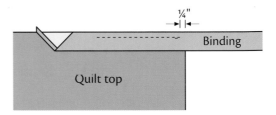

¼"

Binding

Quilt top

8. Turn the quilt so that you will be stitching down the next side. Fold the binding straight up and then back down onto itself, keeping the corner square and the raw edges even. Begin stitching at the edge and stop stitching ¼" from the next corner. Repeat the folding and stitching process at each corner.

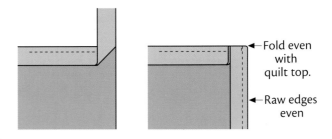

Fold even with quilt top.

Raw edges even

9. Stop stitching about 2" from the starting point of the binding. Trim the end of the binding so it overlaps the beginning about 2", trimming diagonally. Tuck the end of the binding inside the beginning of the binding and finish sewing the binding in place.

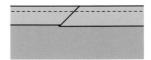

10. Fold the binding over the raw edge of the quilt to the back. Blindstitch the folded edge in place, mitering the corners.

Fold first.

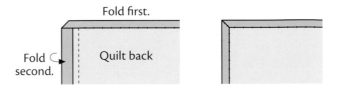

Fold second.

Quilt back

11. Add a label to the back of the quilt. This is a family heirloom, so you want future generations to know about you and the quilt. On your label make sure to include your name and the year you finished the quilt and any special thoughts you had while making it. Your family will truly love knowing all about the maker in years to come.

Adding the Embellishments

1. Apply the hot-fix crystals or beads to blocks 2 and 6, referring to the patterns for placement.
2. For block 4, stitch the seed beads around the edge of the roof, referring to the photo for placement. Apply the hot-fix crystals or beads to the sky around the stars.

3. Refer to the block 5 pattern and to "Sequins" on page 6 to sew the sequins and seed beads to the tree.

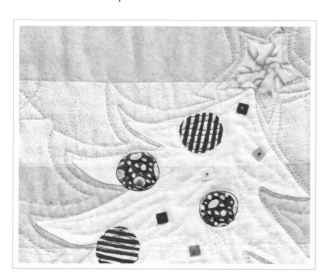

4. For block 7, thread a large-eye needle with six strands of white embroidery floss. Knot one end. On the front of the quilt, insert the needle through the eyelet and bring it to the back, leaving a thread tail about 3" long. Bring the needle from the back to the front, close to the same spot where you first inserted the needle. Cut the thread, leaving another thread tail about 3" long. Tie a knot at the end of this tail, and then tie the tails in a bow. Repeat for the remaining tags.
5. For block 9, cut the red ribbon into three 5" lengths. Thread a length through a large-eye needle. With the needle, go in and out through the center piece of a bow as though you were taking a stitch, making sure you do not go through to the back of the quilt. Pull the ribbon through until you reach the middle of the length. Take the needle off of the ribbon and then pull on both ends to make them even. Tie the ribbon in a double knot. String three jingle bells on the ribbon and then tie it in a double knot again to secure the bells. Repeat for the remaining two bows.

6. Sew the buttons to blocks 10 and 11 where desired, referring to the photo as needed.
7. Refer to "Yo-Yos" on page 7 and use the template on the pullout pattern section to make 78 yo-yos from the assorted fabrics. Pin or glue-baste the yo-yos in place on the border strip, leaving an equal amount of space between each. You will need 20 for each side border and 19 each for the top and bottom borders. Using matching thread, tack the edge of each yo-yo in place, going through the top and batting only.

Appliquéd Felt Stockings

The stockings were hung by the chimney with care . . . . Just that familiar verse can stir up excitement in children of all ages. These stockings are fun and easy to make—you can easily whip up one for each member of the family to enjoy. I've given instructions for making the basic stocking. You can personalize it by using different appliqués and cuff treatments and embellishing however you wish.

Finished size: 10½" x 14½"

Materials

½ yard of 36"-wide wool felt or felted wool for stocking front and back (you will also need ½ yard extra of a contrasting color if you want to make a striped background)

Wool felt or felted wool in assorted colors for appliqués

1 yard of ribbon for cuff embellishment and hanging loop

Assorted buttons, crystals, sequins, and/or beads for embellishing

1 yard of 18"-wide fusible web (optional; for striped background)

1 package of jumbo rickrack for between stocking front and back

1 package of medium rickrack for stocking front

Tracing paper

Pinking shears or wave-edge rotary-cutter blade (optional)

Instructions

The stocking and appliqué patterns are given on pages 1, 3, and 4 of the pullout pattern section.

1. Trace the stocking pattern onto tracing paper. Use the pattern to cut two stocking pieces from the wool felt or felted wool for the front and back with pinking shears or wave-edge rotary-cutter blade if desired. If you want a striped background, follow the manufacturer's instructions to apply fusible web to one side of the contrasting-color wool felt. Cut it into 2"-wide strips and fuse it to the stocking front to create a striped pattern.

2. Apply trim to the top of the stocking front using one of the following options. Cut a piece of ribbon approximately 1" longer than the width of the stocking across the area you want to apply the trim. Turn the ends under ½" and position the ribbon on the stocking front; stitch along both long edges. Or, use the stocking cuff pattern to cut a cuff from felt, cutting the top and side edges with the pinking shears or wave-edge rotary cutter blade if you did that for the stocking edges; embellish with ribbon as described above and then stitch the entire cuff to the top of the stocking, aligning the top and side edges.

3. Refer to "Fusible-Web Appliqué" on page 6 to prepare the desired appliqués from the appropriate felt colors. The Snowman pattern is the reversed image of the one used for block 1 of the quilt. Refer to the photo to include the five hexagon flower appliqués and the row of seven hexagons across the top band, if desired (I made the appliqués from cotton fabric scraps and needle-turn appliquéd them in place but you could use any fabric and any appliqué method), and be sure to reverse the hat pattern.

4. Fuse the appliqués to the stocking front in numerical order. Stitch around the edges of each appliqué shape with a straight stitch or a decorative stitch, whichever you prefer. For the Christmas Tree stocking,

use a narrow zigzag stitch to make the tree stand. For the Snowman stocking, use a narrow zigzag stitch to make the snowman's arms and the flower stems and leaves.

5. Embellish the stocking front with beads, buttons, and/or crystals as desired, keeping them out of the seam allowance.

6. Cut a 4" length of ribbon for the hanging loop. Fold it in half, wrong sides together. Pin the ribbon raw edges to the wrong side of the stocking front at the upper corner on the heel side of the stocking.

7. Pin the jumbo rickrack to the wrong side of the stocking side and bottom edges so that one half is visible from the front side, turning under the raw ends. Baste it in place with thread that matches the felt.

8. Using a ¼" seam allowances, stitch the stocking front and back pieces wrong sides together, leaving the top edge open.

9. Stitch the medium rickrack to the front of the stocking along the edges using matching thread and turning under the raw ends.

Cupcakes for Santa

Your little ones will love making these candy flower cupcakes for Santa and his helpers. Before you frost your cooled cupcakes, cut large gumdrops in half and flatten them with your fingers or a small rolling pin on a flat surface sprinkled with granulated sugar. Frost the cupcakes. While the frosting is still wet, arrange five flattened drops into flower petals around the outside of the cupcake and place a contrasting small gumdrop in the center. Cut flattened green gumdrops into leaf shapes and place one or two on each cupcake between the petals.

The Nights Before Christmas Wall Hanging

This is one of my favorite Christmas memories. One year my mom and dad surprised my sisters and me with a gift for each of the 24 days before Christmas. My sisters and I couldn't wait to wake up each morning and see what was in the little pockets of the wall hanging Mom had made. It would be something like bubble gum, candy, or new crayons or stickers. What fun we had! We chewed more bubble gum that year than three little girls should be allowed.

So here is my version. For the seven days before Christmas, have the children in your family attach one pocket to the bottom of the wall hanging before they go to bed. Your job is to place a surprise for each child in the pocket. It could be a secret note from Santa, a candy treat, or even a map to a bigger treasure.

Finished wall-hanging size: 23" x 39"
(not including hanging pockets)

Materials

¼ yard *each* of 8 assorted fabrics for border and pockets

¼ yard *each* of 3 different white fabrics for the bodies

½ yard of light blue fabric for base of Crazy patch pieces

½ yard of light green fabric for appliquéd center background

¼ yard of fabric for pocket-front lining

1 fat quarter *each* of 2 coordinating fabrics for reversible pocket front/back

Assorted scraps of fabrics for hats, aprons, cat and dog collars, hair bows, cheeks, and carrot noses

½ yard of dark green fabric for binding

1½ yards of fabric for backing

29" x 45" piece of batting

4 yards of 18"-wide fusible web

Embroidery floss: white (optional; for hand embroidering snowflakes), black, brown,

White rayon thread (optional; for machine embroidering snowflakes)

Buttons: 3 small round for Snow Dad; 4 small stars for Snow Boy; medium heart for Snow Mom; small heart for Snow Girl; small square for Snow Baby; 14 round in assorted sizes and colors for top and bottom borders

Assorted beads and crystals

Assorted embroidery thread, pearl cotton, floss, and silk ribbon in blue, light green, pink, turquoise, lavender and red for Crazy patches

Assorted sizes of rickrack and trims including 1 package of white iridescent medium rickrack

Brown, black, and white ultrafine-tip markers

Large-eye sharp embroidery needle

Teflon pressing sheet

Chalk pencil

Tracing paper

Note: The embroidered snowflakes used for the featured project were from the Sparkle Snowflakes embroidery card (970339) from Dakota Collectibles. Visit the company's website at www.gonutsgocreative.com.

Cutting

From the light green fabric, cut:
1 rectangle, 15" x 31"

From the light blue fabric, cut:
4 strips, 5" x 42"

From the dark green fabric, cut:
4 strips, 2½" x 42"

Appliquéing the Center Rectangle

The appliqué patterns and a placement guide are given on page 4 of the pullout pattern section.

1. Refer to "Appliqué Methods" on page 5 to prepare the appliqué shapes from the appropriate fabrics using your preferred method.

2. Fold the light green rectangle in half vertically and horizontally; finger-press the folds to mark the center. Open up the rectangle and appliqué the shapes in place in numerical order.

3. Use the markers to transfer the stitching details to the rectangle, using black for the eyes, mouths, and dog's nose; brown for the arms and fingers; and white for the snowflakes. Refer to "Embroidery Stitches" on page 7 and use two strands of black floss to work French knots for the eyes, mouths, and dog's nose. Use three strands of brown floss to stem stitch the arms and fingers. If you are hand embroidering the snowflakes, use the patterns on page 4 of the pullout pattern section and work them with two strands of white floss and a stem stitch. If you are machine embroidering the snowflakes, use the rayon thread.

4. Trim the rectangle to 13" x 29", keeping the design centered.

Making the Crazy Patch Border Pieces

1. Refer to the manufacturer's instructions to adhere fusible web to the wrong side of each of the eight assorted fabrics for the border and pockets.

2. Using your rotary cutter and long ruler, randomly cut each fabric apart at angles. Remove the paper backing from each piece.

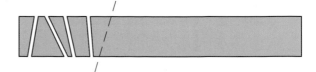

3. Place a light blue strip on your ironing board, right side up. Starting at one end and working toward the other, place a piece you cut in step 2 on the strip, right side up. Continue placing pieces on the strip so that the pieces touch each other, occasionally leaving the blue strip fabric exposed. When you have completely covered the strip and are happy with the arrangement, press the pieces in place *through the center of the strip only*, just to hold them in place. You do not want the fusible to adhere to your ironing board cover. Now, place the Teflon pressing sheet under one edge of the strip and press the pieces in place. Continue moving the pressing sheet under areas that have not been pressed until all of the pieces have been completely fused to the strip. Repeat with the remaining blue strips.

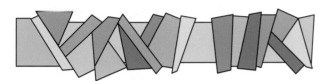

4. Turn each of the fused strips to the wrong side. Using a rotary cuter and ruler, trim the excess fused pieces even with the light blue base border strip. Each strip should measure 5" wide.

5. Embellish the "seams" between each of the patchwork pieces with an assortment of hand embroidery stitches (see "Embroidery Stitches" on page 7), machine embroidery stitches, or trims. Add one embroidered snowflake to each border strip, stitching right over the seam stitches.

Assembling and Quilting the Wall Hanging

1. Apply fusible web to the wrong side of the appliquéd center rectangle and each crazy-patch border strip.

2. Trim the backing fabric to 29" x 45". Lay the backing on your work surface, wrong side up. Tape the edges to the surface so that it is smooth but not stretched.

3. Center the batting over the backing and smooth it out.

4. Peel the paper backing off the center rectangle and center it on the batting; smooth it out. Fuse it in place.

5. Remove the paper backing from the crazy-patch border strips and lay them around the center block, overlapping the edge of the center rectangle ⅛". Let the border ends overlap one another for now. Do not fuse in place yet; if you are using Steam-A-Seam 2, just press the borders in place with your hands, otherwise pin them in place.

6. Working on one corner at a time, use a chalk pencil and your ruler to draw a line from the corner of the center rectangle to the point where the borders intersect each other along the outer edges.

7. Place a pin through the border on each side of the drawn line. Slightly lift up the border pieces so you can get your scissors underneath, and then cut on the marked line, working from the outside edge to the quilt center rectangle. Repeat on each corner. Set the cutaway pieces aside for the pockets. Fuse the borders in place. Pin a piece of rickrack over each of the mitered corner "seams." You will stitch down the rickrack when quilting.

8. Using safety pins, baste the layers together. Quilt the wall hanging. Start quilting in the center and work toward the outer edges. I echo quilted around each snow person and each snowflake. The border was straight stitched close to each of the embroidered lines.

9. Stitch the white iridescent rickrack around the edges of the center rectangle, covering the edges of the rectangle and the inner edges of the border strips at the same time.

10. Bind the wall hanging's edges, referring to steps 5–10 of "Finishing the Quilt" on pages 18–19.

11. Evenly space seven buttons along the each of the top and bottom edges of the wall hanging and stitch them in place.

Making the Pockets

1. Trace the front and back pocket patterns onto the tracing paper and cut them out.

2. Adhere fusible web to the wrong side of both of the fat quarters for the pocket fronts and backs. Fuse the fat quarters, wrong sides together. Use the back pocket pattern to cut out seven pieces from the fused fabric square. Embroider a snowflake on one side of four of the pieces and on the opposite side of the remaining three pieces, placing the embroidery near the top so that it will be visible once the front pieces are sewn in place. Refer to the photo if necessary.

3. Fuse the Crazy patch pieces that were left over from the border strips to the wrong side of the pocket-front lining fabric. The pieces already have fusible applied. Use the front pocket pattern to cut out seven front pieces from the fused Crazy patch pieces, flipping the pattern over after you cut four pieces so that the remaining three pieces will be angled in the opposite direction.

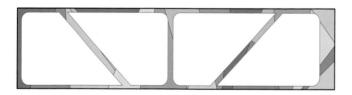

4. Referring to the photo, lay out the pocket back pieces side by side so that the colors alternate. The snowflake embroidery should be facing up on each piece. Place a front piece over each back piece, alternating the angled edge of every other piece.

5. Working on one front and back set at a time, stitch a length of rickrack to the angled edge of each front pocket piece using matching or clear thread. Lay the front pocket piece back on the back piece and stitch them together about 1/8" from the front pocket edges, leaving the angled edge open. Sew the same color rickrack to the edges of the joined pocket pieces, starting and stopping along the bottom edge. Cut a 5" length of rickrack and fold it in half to make a loop. Stitch the loop ends to the back of the pocket at the point. Repeat for the remaining sets of pocket pieces.

6. Add the buttons to the snow people. Apply any desired beads, crystals, buttons or other embellishments to the wall hanging and pockets.

7. Hang the pockets from the buttons at the bottom of the wall hanging.

Candy Cane Table Runner

Dressing up your table for the holiday season is part of the fun of Christmas. I like to deck the dining room table with a more formal covering and give the kitchen table a more playful look. This table runner is perfect for any table and can be made quickly and easily with fusible appliqué. The whimsical yo-yo border adds the final touch.

Finished table-runner size: 15" x 72"

Materials

1⅜ yards *total* of assorted fabrics for yo-yos
1 yard of blue fabric for appliquéd center background
1 yard of white fabric for candy canes and Pinwheel blocks
1 yard *total* of 4 assorted red fabrics for candy canes and Pinwheel blocks
¾ yard of medium green fabric for bows
Scrap of light green fabric for bow centers
1¼ yards of fabric for backing
½ yard of green fabric for binding
21" x 78" piece of batting
2 yards of 18"-wide fusible web
2 packages of white medium rickrack

Cutting

From the blue fabric, cut:
2 strips, 9½" x 33½"

From the assorted red fabrics, cut a *total* of:
14 strips, 2½" x 21"

From the white fabric, cut:
7 strips, 2½" x 42"; cut each strip in half crosswise to yield 14 strips, 2½" x 21"

From the green fabric for binding, cut:
5 strips, 2½" x 42"

Appliquéing the Center Rectangle

The appliqué patterns are given on page 3 of the pullout pattern section.

1. Sew the blue rectangles together along the short ends to make one long piece, 9½" x 66½".
2. Refer to "Fusible-Web Appliqué" on page 6 to prepare the appliqué shapes from the appropriate fabrics. You will need five of each candy cane piece and five of each bow piece, reversing three of each.
3. Arrange the candy cane and bow appliqués on the blue rectangle in numerical order, reversing every other complete candy cane motif. Position the motifs so there is an equal amount of space between each candy cane and an equal amount of space at the ends.

Making the Pinwheel Blocks

1. Pair each red strip with a white strip, right sides together with the white strip on top. Crosscut the layered strips into 108 squares, 2½" x 2½". Keep the layered squares together.
2. Using a ruler and a sharp pencil or ultrafine-tip permanent marker, draw a diagonal line from corner to corner on each white square. Stitch ¼" from each side of the marked lines. Cut the squares apart on the drawn lines to make 216 half-square-triangle units. Press the seam allowances toward the red fabric. Trim off the dog-ears.

Make 216.

3. Arrange four half-square triangle units into two rows of two units each as shown. Sew the units in each row together, and then join the rows. Repeat to make a total of 54 Pinwheel blocks. Square up the blocks to 3½" x 3½".

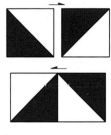 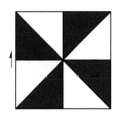

Make 54.

4. Sew 22 Pinwheel blocks together end to end to make a side border. Repeat to make a total of two borders. Sew these borders to the sides of the appliquéd quilt center. Sew five Pinwheel blocks together end to end to make an end border. Repeat to make a total of two borders. Join these borders to the ends of the quilt center.

Finishing the Table Runner

1. Piece the quilt backing so that it is 4" to 6" longer and wider than the quilt top. Layer the quilt top with batting and backing; baste the layers together. Hand or machine quilt as desired. Trim the batting and backing even with the quilt top. Bind the quilt edges, referring to steps 5–10 of "Finishing the Quilt" on pages 18–19.
2. Refer to "Yo-Yos" on page 7 and use the template on the pullout pattern section to make 120 yo-yos from the assorted fabrics.
3. Hand whipstitch (see page 7) the first yo-yo to one corner of the binding. Make a knot, but don't cut the thread. Move the needle through the first yo-yo, bringing the needle out where the next yo-yo will be touching the side of the first yo-yo. Whipstitch the second yo-yo to the first one, then move the needle and thread through the second yo-yo to attach it to the binding edge. Make a knot, but don't cut the thread. Continue adding yo-yos in the same manner until you have sewn 50 to each side of the table runner (corner to corner) and 10 to each end.

Snowflake Pillows

The weather outside may be frightful, but you can still enjoy the flakes while you're all comfy and warm inside by sprinkling these quick-to-make pillows throughout the house.

Finished size: 12" x 12"

Materials (for one pillow)

½ yard of dark- to medium-colored 36"-wide wool felt or felted wool for pillow front and back

½ yard of white wool felt for snowflake and scalloped edge

Hot-fix crystals or beads (optional)

½ yard of 18"-wide fusible web

12" pillow form

White 30-weight rayon thread

Freezer paper

Appliquéing the Pillow Front

The appliqué patterns for the snowflakes and the scalloped border pieces are given on pages 1, 2, and 4 of the pull-out pattern section. The snowflake patterns shown on the blue pillows in the photograph use the basic shapes from blocks 2 and 6 of the main quilt; the snowflake pattern for the green pillow is given separately.

1. From the dark- to medium-colored wool felt or felted wool, cut two squares, 12½" x 12½", for the pillow front and back. Fold the front square in half vertically and horizontally and press the folds with an iron to mark the center.

2. Follow the manufacturer's instructions to adhere the fusible web to the wrong side of the white wool felt or felted wool. Do not remove the paper backing.

3. Trace the desired snowflake pattern with any desired changes onto the dull side of a piece of freezer paper and cut out the pieces. Iron the freezer paper pieces to the right side of the white wool felt or felted wool. Cut out the appliqué pieces. Remove the freezer-paper patterns and the fusible-web paper backing from the appliqué pieces.

4. Center the main snowflake appliqué on the pillow front square and fuse it in place. Position the remaining appliqués and fuse them in place.

5. Using the white thread and a narrow zigzag stitch, stitch around each appliqué.

Adding the Scalloped Edge

1. From the white wool felt or felted wool, cut two 10" x 12" rectangles. Apply fusible web to the wrong side of one of the rectangles. Lay the remaining rectangle over the fusible web side of the first rectangle and fuse them together. Cut the fused rectangle into four strips, 1½" x 12".

2. Trace the scallop pattern onto the dull side of a piece of freezer paper and cut it out. Using the freezer-paper template, cut out 28 scallops from the fused strips.

3. With the white thread and a narrow zigzag stitch, stitch around the curved edges of each scallop.

4. Evenly space seven scallops on each side of the pillow front, placing the first and last scallops ¼" from the ends. The rounded edge of the scallops should be pointing toward the center of the pillow. Baste the scallops in place ¼" from the pillow edges.

5. Pin the pillow front and back right sides together. Sew ¼" from the pillow edges, leaving an opening for turning and inserting the pillow form. Be careful not to catch the scallop edges at the corners. Turn the pillow right side out. Add any desired embellishments to the pillow front. Insert the pillow form through the opening. Hand stitch the opening closed.

Leave opening for turning.

About the Author

Melinda has sewn since she was a little girl and made her first quilt at the age of 19. Her background is in art and design, and she is a true artist at heart.

When she wants to paint, she creates her fabulous fusible flower quilts that are like paintings, but made only from fabric and thread—no paint. She has won numerous awards with her technique, which is featured in *Cutting-Garden Quilts* (Martingale & Company, 2007).

Melinda finds nothing as enjoyable as sitting down and making a traditional appliquéd quilt. She is known for her color palette and style of design and loves to take her designs and turn them into patterns. You can see more of her artwork and designs at www.melindabula.com.